はしがき

　本書は、Voice of America（VOA）の Special English から特に健康と環境分野を扱っている素材を厳選して英語教材としたものです。
　この教材で取り上げられているトピックは身近なものから世界規模のものまでと幅広く、学生の皆さんも飽きることなく興味を持って学習を継続できる、リスニング力養成に最適な教材です。
　VOA Special English は非英語話者対象に放送されている Authentic Material であり、取り上げられているトピックは最新のニュースです。Special English のニュースはナチュラルスピードの 3 分の 2 の速度で読まれていますが、不自然なものではなく、リスニング力の養成に適しています。本書付属の CD には、実際に放送された音声だけでなく、ネイティブ・スピーカーによってナチュラルスピードで吹き替えられた音声も収録されています。Special English の基本使用語彙は 1,500 語程度ですが、それ以外の語には Notes に解説を付けています。
　本書は、Pre-listening、While-listening、Post-listening の各段階で、語彙、大意把握、内容把握、イディオム確認、英語表現のタスクを課しています。
　Title・関連写真：ユニットのタイトルや関連写真によって、トピック内容に対する学生の皆さんのスキーマ（背景知識）を活性化し、トピック内容の理解に対する動機付けとなります。
　Vocabulary：本文中の語の語義としてふさわしい定義を選択します。英語を英語で理解することによってトピックの内容理解への手がかりが得られることになります。
　Summary Check：1st Listening の後、ここでトピック内容の大まかな概要を把握して下さい。
　2nd Listening：本文中の空所に聴き取った語を入れることによって細かな内容理解を確認します。空所箇所は、トピック内容のキーワードを中心に、聴き取りにくい箇所にも設定しています。
　True or False?：トピック内容の把握についてその正誤を確認します。
　Vocabulary Building：本文中の語の意味や使い方をより発展的に理解するのを助けます。
　Useful Expressions：一般的な表現の中で本文に出現したイディオムの確認を行います。
　Translations：Vocabulary で取り上げた語句の並べ替えによる英作文を行います。トピック内容に関連するものとなっています。
　付属 CD：リスニング活動は授業中だけでなく授業以外でも自主的に取り組むことが必要です。この付属 CD を十分に活用して下さい。
　本書を用いた学習と並行して VOA のサイト（http://www.voanews.com）へアクセスして最新のニュースを視聴されることをお勧めします。
　最後になりますが、本書の出版をお勧め頂いた松柏社社長森信久氏に対して心から御礼を申し上げます。

安浪誠祐
Richard S. Lavin

本教材のシリーズには、以下のタイトルがございます。

『健康と環境：身近なトピックから国際問題まで』
The Global Topics of Health and Environment from VOA（2006）
『世界の健康と環境：日常生活から国際的課題まで』
World Reports of Health and Environment from VOA（2008）
『VOA に見る健康と環境——アレルギーの原因から地球環境問題まで』
A Look at Global Health & Environment with VOA（2009）
『VOA で知る健康と環境——屋上菜園から牛ゲノム解読まで』
Health & Environment from VOA: How Everyday Life Affects Global Issues（2010）
『健康と環境を知る——〈塩分と健康の関係〉から〈遺伝子組み換え作物と環境〉まで』
Global Health & Environment: VOA Topics from Around the World（2011）
『VOA：睡眠障害の原因からチッ素排出量の現状まで』
From Daily Topics to World Issues: Health & Environment from VOA（2012）
『未来につながる健康と環境』
To the Future: Topics in Health & Environment from VOA（2013）
『VOA の健康＆環境レポートで世界を知る——オランウータン向けアプリの開発から天候の予測まで』
Closer to the World: VOA's Health & Environment Reports（2014）

Contents

1. カフェインは記憶力を増大させる？
   Don't Forget Your Coffee! [1]

2. 南アフリカが造る
   ソーラーカーの未来
   Solar Cars in South Africa [5]

3. 失読症の人は
   テレビゲームに速く反応できる？
   Video Games and Dyslexia [9]

4. ヘルシーフードを作る栽培方法
   Let's Go Fishing...and Farming! [13]

5. 音が脳機能を高める？
   Scientists Get with the Beat [17]

6. クリスマスツリーは
   自然の木が良い？
   Farmed Christmas Trees:
   Good for the Environment? [21]

7. タンパク質がHIVから
   赤ん坊を救う？
   Can Mothers' Milk Beat HIV? [25]

8. 太陽エネルギーの有効利用
   The World's Largest Solar Power
   Plant [29]

9. 統合失調症には在宅治療が
   効果的？
   Is Community-Based Mental
   Health Treatment Better? [33]

10. 農業とソーシャルメディア
    How Can Farmers Use Social
    Media? [37]

11. いかに子供たちの食料供給を
    増やすか
    How Can We Get Children to Eat
    Better? [41]

12. 農業による環境汚染を
    減らす方法
    Making Agriculture Sustainable
    [45]

13. ダイエットは虫歯の原因になる？
    Diet at the Root of Tooth Decay?
    [49]

14. エタノールとトウモロコシの
    意外な関係
    Concerns about Ethanol [53]

15. 新たなマラリア診断法
    A New Way to Find Malaria
    Infections [57]

1 Don't Forget Your Coffee!

カフェインは記憶力を増大させる？

VOCABULARY

(a) 〜 (e) のなかから語義としてふさわしいものをそれぞれ選びなさい。

1) tea   2) caffeine   3) memory
4) inactive   5) pill

(a) a substance in some plants that stimulates the nervous system

(b) similar to a tablet, usually containing medicine

(c) a drink made from the leaves of the *Camellia sinensis* plant

(d) not having any effect in the body

(e) the ability to keep information in the mind

 1st Listening ▶▶▶ まず VOA ニュースを聴きましょう。

SUMMARY CHECK

ニュースの概要として最もふさわしいものを下の 1) 〜 4) のなかから選びなさい。

1) Drinking more than one cup of coffee a day is bad for the memory.
2) Caffeine may improve long-term memory.
3) Mike Yassa wants to move to the University of California.
4) *Nature Neuroscience* is a journal published in Irvine.

2nd Listening

▶▶▶ もう一回 VOA ニュースを聴き、(　　) を埋めましょう。

From VOA Learning English, this is the Health Report.

Many people say they cannot start their day without (1.　　　) having a cup of coffee or tea. People say these drinks help them think clearly and feel (2.　　　).

This is because of caffeine, a substance (3.　　　) in some plants. Caffeine helps to give a jump start to the nervous (4.　　　). Now a report says it may also improve long-term memory.

The report was (5.　　　) in the journal *Nature Neuroscience*. Mike Yassa is (6.　　　) the University of California in Irvine. He and other researchers wanted to know if caffeine could improve what they called memory consolidation. They asked a group of (7.　　　) to learn something new. Then, the same people were (8.　　　) caffeine, the active ingredient in coffee, tea and chocolate. The research team studied 160 people who were caffeine-free.

On the first day, these people were (9.　　　) pictures of everyday objects. They were asked to (10.　　　) whether the pictures could be found inside the house or (11.　　　). Some people were then given a pill with caffeine. The (12.　　　) were given a placebo—a pill (13.　　　) an inactive substance.

On the second day, all of the (14.　　　) were asked to look at more pictures. Some of the images were (15.　　　) like the ones they had seen 24 hours (16.　　　). But other images were different. Individuals taking the caffeine pills had a 10 to 12 percent increase in their ability to remember objects. The (17.　　　) of caffeine used in the study was (18.　　　) to a strong cup of coffee.

Mr. Yassa says pills with a little more caffeine also increased memory, but (19.　　　) in some people (20.　　　) more nervous.

For VOA Learning English, I'm Carolyn Presutti.

Notes

☐ substance 物質　　☐ *Nature Neuroscience*『ネーチャー・ニューロサイエンス』誌
☐ University of California in Irvine カリフォルニア大学アーバイン校
☐ memory consolidation 記憶の固定　　☐ active ingredient 有効成分　　☐ pill 錠剤
☐ placebo 偽薬（薬効はなく、実験の際に対照剤として与える）　　☐ subject 被験者

TRUE OR FALSE?

1) 〜 5) のなかからニュースの内容として正しいものにはT、間違っているものにはFを選びなさい。

1) The effects of tea and coffee in making people feel awake are imaginary.
2) Mike Yassa was involved with the study reported in the unit.
3) Some of the people in the study were given a placebo.
4) People who took caffeine pills remembered pictures better a day later.
5) People who took a higher dose of caffeine remembered less.

VOCABULARY BUILDING

下の語群の語を本文中で探して下線を引きなさい。そして、下の1) 〜 8) の英文の意味が通るように品詞・形などを変えたものを入れなさい。

1) Human and ape DNA have many _____.
2) _____ of many words is important when you want to communicate in a foreign language.
3) Recent _____ has shown that coffee may have several health benefits.
4) Are you _____ to come to tomorrow's party?
5) _____ numbers of people in developed nations are becoming obese.
6) Making the time to get enough exercise when you are young has many _____ benefits.
7) The company grew rapidly for five years then entered a period of _____.
8) This cake has many delicious _____ such as brown sugar, butter, and chocolate chips.

ability	consolidation	increase	know
long-term	researchers	similar	ingredients

[3]

USEFUL EXPRESSIONS

日本語に合うように（　　）を埋めなさい。

1) 先ずビザを取らなければ訪問できない国もある。

   It is not possible to visit some countries (   ) first obtaining a visa.

2) トラックやバスの運転手の中にはコーヒーをたくさん飲んで、常に注意して事故に遭わないようにする者もいる。

   Some truck and bus drivers drink lots of coffee to help (   ) stay alert and avoid accidents.

3) 映画『黄色いハンカチーフ』では、一人の男が出所して妻が今でも自分を愛しているかどうかを確かめるために彼女に会いに行く。

   In the movie *The Yellow Handkerchief*, a man leaves prison and goes to see his wife to find out (   ) she still loves him.

4) 多くのアメリカの家族は冬の季節の終わりにいわゆる spring cleaning（春の大掃除）をする。

   Many American families do (   ) they call spring cleaning at the end of the winter season.

TRANSLATIONS

日本語に合うように（　　）の語句を並び替えて、一文を完成させなさい。

1) 睡眠の主な機能の一つは長期記憶における情報の体系化であると考えられる。

   One of the primary functions of sleep (be / in / information / is / long-term / memory / of / the organizing / thought / to).

   ....

2) ほとんどの調合薬には活性成分に加えていくつかの非活性成分が含まれている。

   Most pharmaceutical drugs (active / addition / contain / in / inactive / ingredient / ingredients / several / the / to).

   ....

2 Solar Cars in South Africa

南アフリカが造るソーラーカーの未来

VOCABULARY

(a) ～ (e) のなかから語義としてふさわしいものをそれぞれ選びなさい。

1) solar   2) countryside   3) vehicle

4) coal   5) project

(a) related to the sun

(b) something used to transport people or things

(c) a black substance used as fuel

(d) a planned piece of work with a specific purpose

(e) an area that is far from towns and cities

 1st Listening ▶▶▶ まず VOA ニュースを聴きましょう。

SUMMARY CHECK

ニュースの概要として最もふさわしいものを下の 1) ～ 4) のなかから選びなさい。

1) The University of Johannesburg has a solar car project and other alternative energy projects.

2) Warren Larter recently became a director of the University of Johannesburg.

3) Kegan Smith is a former student, a former manager, and a current lecturer at the University of Johannesburg.

4) The University of Johannesburg's solar-powered car weighs 300 kilograms.

2nd Listening
▶▶▶ もう一回 VOA ニュースを聴き、(　　) を埋めましょう。

From VOA Learning English, this is the Technology Report.

Students in South Africa are building solar-powered cars and (1.   ) them in competitions. The University of Johannesburg is training the students to become (2.   ) on energy. Their 300-kilogram solar-powered car can (3.   ) at a speed of more than 100 kilometers an hour (4.   ) the countryside. The car uses (5.   ) electric power than a coffee maker or food processor.

The young engineers who built the vehicle (6.   ) it in a racing event called the Solar Challenge. The race is for vehicles that use alternative (7.   ) of energy.

Kegan Smith is a former manager of the project, and a (8.   ) at the University of Johannesburg. He says the university wants the students to learn about green energies using (9.   ) examples. He is (10.   ) that the continued use of coal, natural gas and oil will (11.   ) the planet.

When Kegan Smith was a student in 2010, he was part of a group that built an alternative-energy-powered car. Since then, students have built more cars, using (12.   ) hydrogen and energy from the sun.

Warren Larter is currently (13.   ) the university's solar car project. He says solar-powered cars (14.   ) an important learning tool to help students develop new technologies. He (15.   ) a business that lets students work on real-life projects (16.   ) by industry demand. Mr. Larter says the energy market is changing. He says there is a lack of experts (17.   ) in non-traditional energy sources and in solar technology.

Warren Larter and his students are (18.   ) on a car to enter in the next Solar Challenge, in August 2014. They want to (19.   ) the South African race and then (20.   ) internationally.

For VOA Learning English, I'm Alex Villarreal.

Notes

☐ University of Johannesburg ヨハネスバーグ大学　　☐ alternative 代わりの
☐ green energy 自然エネルギー　　☐ hydrogen 水素

TRUE OR FALSE?

1)〜5)のなかからニュースの内容として正しいものにはT、間違っているものにはFを選びなさい。

1) The solar-powered car developed by students at the University of Johannesburg weighs 100 kilograms.

2) A coffee maker uses more electricity than the car developed by the students.

3) Kegan Smith is a former lecturer at the University of Johannesburg.

4) Kegan Smith thinks that expertise in green energies is important for the environment.

5) Warren Larter's business lets students work on real-life energy projects.

VOCABULARY BUILDING

下の語群の語を本文中で探して下線を引きなさい。そして、下の1)〜8)の英文の意味が通るように品詞・形などを変えたものを入れなさい。

1) He is good, but he cannot _____ with the top runners.

2) What is the architect going to _____ next?

3) In order to do well in college, you need to _____ hard.

4) In the long run, we cannot defeat _____.

5) A lack of access to clean water is a big challenge to _____.

6) Universities need to _____ students to be creative problem-solvers.

7) Most functions of an advanced society depend on _____ power.

8) When you cannot solve a problem in one way, try some _____ ways.

| alternative | built | competition | develop |
| electric | natural | student | training |

USEFUL EXPRESSIONS

日本語に合うように（　　　）を埋めなさい。

1) 非常に多くの学生がこの面白いプロジェクトに参加したいと思っていることが私はうれしい。

   I am delighted that so many students want to be (　　　) of this exciting project.

2) 化学の高度な知識と外国語の流暢さをあわせ持つ人が不足している。

   There is a (　　　) of people with advanced knowledge of science and also fluency in a foreign language.

3) コンピュータサイエンスの専門家は高度情報社会で引っ張りだこだ。

   Experts (　　　) computer science are much in demand in our high-tech society.

4) 一週間近くこのエッセーに取り組んでいるが、書き終えることができない。

   I've been (　　　) on this essay for nearly a week but I cannot finish it.

TRANSLATIONS

日本語に合うように（　　　）の語句を並び替えて、一文を完成させなさい。

1) 太陽エネルギーとその他の代替エネルギーは電気を供給するのにますます重要な役割を果たすと期待されている。

   Solar power and other alternative energies (an / are / electricity / expected / important / in / increasingly / play / role / supplying / to).

   ....

2) 多くの国の農業問題は人々が都市に住むために田舎を離れることである。

   A problem for farming in many countries (are / areas / in / is / leaving / live / people / that / the countryside / to / urban).

   ....

3 | Video Games and Dyslexia

失読症の人は
テレビゲームに速く反応できる？

VOCABULARY

(a) ～ (e) のなかから語義としてふさわしいものをそれぞれ選びなさい。

1) population   2) biology   3) volunteer

4) reaction   5) video

(a) moving pictures

(b) all the people in a country or area

(c) someone who does some work without payment

(d) a response to an action

(e) the study of living things

1st Listening ▶▶▶ まず VOA ニュースを聴きましょう。

SUMMARY CHECK

ニュースの概要として最もふさわしいものを下の 1) ～ 4) のなかから選びなさい。

1) A study suggests that dyslexics have trouble redirecting their attention between senses.

2) *Current Biology* is the best source for information on dyslexia.

3) A research center at the University of Oxford is looking to deepen our knowledge of dyslexia.

4) Dyslexia is a learning disorder.

2nd Listening

▶▶▶ もう一回 VOA ニュースを聴き、(　　　) を埋めましょう。

From VOA Learning English, this is the Technology Report.

Dyslexia is a learning (1.　　　). It interferes with the ability to (2.　　　) words and, for some people, to understand what they have (3.　　　). Experts say dyslexia affects about 5 to 10 percent of the population in the United States.

Researchers have (4.　　　) known that people with dyslexia write or read words and letters backwards, in the (5.　　　) order. But a new study shows that dyslexic people may have trouble (6.　　　) their attention between senses. It suggests that such individuals may have trouble moving quickly from what they read to what they (7.　　　).

The findings were published in the journal *Current Biology*. Vanessa Harrar of Britain's University of Oxford led the study. She (8.　　　) 17 people with dyslexia and 19 others without any reading problems. The volunteers were asked to push a (9.　　　) as quickly as possible when they heard a sound, saw a light or (10.　　　) both together. Dr. Harrar (11.　　　) the speed of their reactions.

She found that people with dyslexia were just as (12.　　　) as the others when they saw only a picture or heard only a sound. But the dyslexics had a (13.　　　) reaction time when they heard a sound and saw a picture at the (14.　　　) time.

Dr. Harrar thinks that (15.　　　) action video games could help dyslexic people move more quickly from seeing to hearing. She (16.　　　) that fast moving images in video games (17.　　　) the eyes to move quickly. She says the games train the (18.　　　) system to move quickly.

The study also showed that dyslexic people (19.　　　) learn more quickly if they heard the sound of a letter or word before seeing it. This may affect how dyslexic children are (20.　　　) to read.

For VOA Learning English, I'm Laurel Bowman.

Notes
☐ dyslexia 失読症　　☐ backwards 逆に　　☐ dyslexic 失読症の（人）
☐ *Current Biology*『カレント・バイオロジー』誌　　☐ University of Oxford オックスフォード大学

■ TRUE OR FALSE?

1)～5) のなかからニュースの内容として正しいものにはT、間違っているものにはFを選びなさい。

1) Most people in the United States are affected by dyslexia.

2) A study led by Vanessa Harrar found that dyslexics may find it difficult to move their attention quickly from what they read to what they hear.

3) In an experiment, dyslexics had slower reaction times when they heard a sound and saw a picture at the same time.

4) Vanessa Harrar believes that playing video games could worsen dyslexic people's attention difficulties.

5) The study suggested that dyslexic people learning to read should see the letters or words but not hear them.

■ VOCABULARY BUILDING

下の語群の語を本文中で探して下線を引きなさい。そして、下の1)～8) の英文の意味が通るように品詞・形などを変えたものを入れなさい。

1) The current world _____ is said to be over seven billion people.

2) Many medical _____ are working to find effective treatments for cancer.

3) You won't get many points in the test if you give too many _____ answers.

4) Getting used to fast-moving _____ in video games can be very useful for dyslexic people.

5) _____ something can be a good way to learn it better yourself.

6) Alcohol _____ with the ability to think clearly.

7) I was spending so much money on buses that my friend _____ I move to an apartment nearer the university.

8) Please pay _____ to the instructions.

| attention | images | interferes | population |
| researchers | suggests | taught | wrong |

[11]

USEFUL EXPRESSIONS

日本語に合うように（　　　）を埋めなさい。

1) 不安は外国語の授業で成績がよい人の能力を妨げることがある。

   Anxiety can (　　　) with people's ability to do well in foreign language classes.

2) ネパールでハイキングすることを楽しみにしていたが、高地で呼吸するのは大変だった。

   I was looking forward to hiking in Nepal but I had a lot of (　　　) breathing in the high altitudes.

3) 私たちはできるだけ早く地球の温暖化に対して断固たる行動をとる必要がある。

   We need to take decisive action against global warming as soon as (　　　).

4) あの選手はとてもおとなしく、あまり知られていないチームでプレーしているが、実際にはメッシにだって勝るとも劣らない。

   That player is very quiet and plays for an obscure team but actually he is (　　　) as good as Messi.

TRANSLATIONS

日本語に合うように（　　　）の語句を並び替えて、一文を完成させなさい。

1) 世界の人口は今世紀末までには110億人に達するまで増え続けると見込まれている。

   The global population (by / continue / expected / grow / is / of / the end / the century / to / to / to reach / 11 billion).

   ....

2) 最近、インターネットで音声や映像の素材を使って幅広い科目について学ぶことが可能だ。

   These days, (a wide / about / audio and video / is / it / learn / materials / of / possible / range / subjects / to / using) on the Internet.

   ....

4 Let's Go Fishing ...and Farming!

ヘルシーフードを作る栽培方法

VOCABULARY

(a) ～ (e) のなかから語義としてふさわしいものをそれぞれ選びなさい。

1) efficient   2) nearby   3) nutrient
4) root   5) species

(a) not far away

(b) effective and not using many resources

(c) the part of something that is beneath the soil

(d) a substance that supports health

(e) types of living things

1st Listening ▶▶▶ まず VOA ニュースを聴きましょう。

SUMMARY CHECK

ニュースの概要として最もふさわしいものを下の 1) ～ 4) のなかから選びなさい。

1) There are more than 200 fish in a fish tank at Cylburn Aquaponics Farm.

2) Dave Love, Ellen Perlman, and Laura Genello will be key people in future aquaponics developments.

3) Waste from fish farms causes pollution.

4) Aquaponics combines aquaculture and hydroponics and is a promising way to produce healthy food.

2nd Listening

▶▶▶ もう一回 VOA ニュースを聴き、(　　　) を埋めましょう。

From VOA Learning English, this is the Agriculture Report.

Aquaponics is a new farming (1.　　　) that combines growing vegetables and (2.　　　) fish. The word aquaponics comes from aquaculture and hydroponics. Aquaculture means fish farming. Hydroponics means growing plants in water without soil. Supporters say this is an (3.　　　) way to produce healthy food.

At Cylburn Aquaponics Farm in Baltimore, Maryland, more than two hundred fish swim in a (4.　　　) called a fish tank. The tank water is rich with fish (5.　　　). That water flows through a system that (6.　　　) or cleans it. Then, it flows into nearby tanks where vegetables grow. All of the farm's plants are grown (7.　　　) in the treated water from the fish tanks.

Farm manager Laura Genello says that the fish (8.　　　) all the nutrients the vegetables need. The roots of the plants in turn clean the water for the fish. The (9.　　　) farm produces about 5 to 10 kilograms of vegetables a week. Ms. Genello (10.　　　) to raise about 250 kilograms of fish a year.

Environmentalists (11.　　　) aquaponics because fishing (12.　　　) many wild species. At least half of the world's food fish are produced on farms. Waste from fish farms (13.　　　) pollution.

Dave Love is a researcher at Johns Hopkins University. He (14.　　　) that there are fewer and fewer fish in the ocean. He says fish farming and the waste it produces will (15.　　　).

Ellen Perlman (16.　　　) an aquaponics farm also near Baltimore. Her fish tanks need to be (17.　　　) when the temperature drops. That (18.　　　) money. It is one reason Ms. Perlman has not yet made a (19.　　　).

Back at Cylburn, Laura Genello notes that aquaponics is still new and still needs (20.　　　).

For VOA Learning English, I'm Laurel Bowman.

Notes

- aquaponics アクアポニックス
- aquaculture 水産養殖
- hydroponics 水栽培
- Cylburn Aquaponics Farm シルバーン・アクアポニックス・ファーム
- environmentalist 環境問題専門家
- Johns Hopkins University ジョンズ・ホプキンズ大学

TRUE OR FALSE?

1) 〜 5) のなかからニュースの内容として正しいものには T、間違っているものには F を選びなさい。

1) Aquaculture means growing plants in water without soil.

2) Aquaponics is said to be an efficient way to produce healthy food.

3) At an aquaponics farm, vegetables are grown in treated water from fish tanks.

4) The Cylburn Aquaponics Farm produces about 250 kg of vegetables each week.

5) Fish farms cause some environmental problems.

VOCABULARY BUILDING

下の語群の語を本文中で探して下線を引きなさい。そして、下の 1) 〜 8) の英文の意味が通るように品詞・形などを変えたものを入れなさい。

1) Healthy _____ usually means healthy crops.

2) The river _____ through the valley.

3) It is estimated that the number of _____ of living things on Earth is about 8.7 million.

4) Environmentalists are looking for ways to reduce _____.

5) An air conditioner is used to control the _____ in a room.

6) Email is an _____ way to contact people.

7) Our drinking water is _____ to remove impurities.

8) In Europe, many people living in large cities like to _____ vegetables in a garden in the suburbs.

| efficient | filters | flows | grow |
| soil | species | temperature | waste |

USEFUL EXPRESSIONS

日本語に合うように（　　　）を埋めなさい。

1) 「ブランチ」は朝食と昼食に由来していて、ある国では週末にはとても一般的だ。

   "Brunch" (　　　　) from breakfast and lunch and is quite popular in some countries on weekends.

2) その音楽は上手く演奏されていて情緒豊かだった。

   The music was well-performed and (　　　　) with emotion.

3) 食べ過ぎと運動不足は体重増加の原因となる可能性があり、今度はそれが多くの他の病気を引き起こす可能性がある。

   Overeating and lack of exercise can cause gains in weight, and that in (　　　) can cause many other disorders.

4) 最近、退職するまで最初の仕事を続ける人がますます少なくなっている。

   These days, there are (　　　　) and fewer people who continue at their first job until retirement.

TRANSLATIONS

日本語に合うように（　　　）の語句を並び替えて、一文を完成させなさい。

1) 現在のところ、野生生物の 18,000 以上の種は自然の生息地の破壊が原因で絶滅の危機にあると言われている。

   At present, more than 18,000 species (are / at / be / because / extinction / of / of / of / of / risk / said / the destruction / to / wildlife) their natural habitats.

   ....

2) 人が健康な生活を送るのに必要とされる栄養素にはタンパク質や多くのビタミンやミネラルが含まれる。

   Nutrients (a healthy / by / humans / include / life / live / protein / required / to) and many vitamins and minerals.

   ....

5 | Scientists Get with the Beat

音が脳機能を高める？

VOCABULARY

(a) 〜 (e) のなかから語義としてふさわしいものをそれぞれ選びなさい。

1) neurological   2) former   3) device

4) temperature   5) disease

(a) an illness or disorder

(b) a measure of heat

(c) a thing that is made for a particular purpose

(d) past; from before

(e) related to the nervous system

1st Listening ▶▶▶ まず VOA ニュースを聴きましょう。

SUMMARY CHECK

ニュースの概要として最もふさわしいものを下の 1) 〜 4) のなかから選びなさい。

1) Mickey Hart, although retired from The Grateful Dead, can still play the drums rhythmically.

2) Research with rock musicians may be helpful in understanding music and rhythm more deeply.

3) Mickey Hart's grandmother wanted to join The Grateful Dead but was not able to do so.

4) Rhythm may help people with neurological diseases to lead a better life.

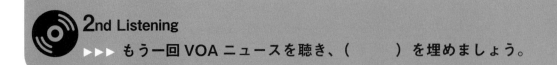

From VOA Learning English, this is the Health Report.

American researchers say contact with (1.   ) may help people with neurological diseases (2.   ) a better life. The researchers reported the finding after they (3.   ) out experiments with a famous rock and roll (4.   ).

Scientists say timing has a (5.   ) influence on how the human brain works. And when the timing is off, so is the (6.   ) of information.

The new study was the work of researchers at the University of California, San Francisco. They (7.   ) the brain of Mickey Hart. He is a (8.   ) member of the rock group the Grateful Dead. For the study he was (9.   ) to play electronic drums as part of a computer game. The experiments (10.   ) neuroscience with modern technology, gaming and the (11.   ) world. Mickey Hart (12.   ) sensor devices on his head as he played the drums. In another room, scientists watched how his brain (13.   ) to the orderly beat of rhythm. They watched how his eyes moved. They (14.   ) changes in his blood flow and body temperature. All this information showed his brain's (15.   ) in real time.

Mickey Hart is interested in (16.   ) how his brain, what he calls the "Master Clock," works. He has also been interested for years in the power of music. In the 1980s, he used music to (17.   ) with his grandmother who was suffering from Alzheimer's disease. She had not (18.   ) in a year. When he played the drums, she spoke his name and started talking again.

Scientists say their (19.   ) is to use rhythm training and even video games to improve brain function. They believe that when the brain operates correctly, people enjoy a better (20.   ) of life.

For VOA Learning English, I'm Alex Villareal.

Notes
☐ University of California, San Francisco カリフォルニア大学サンフランシスコ校
☐ the Grateful Dead グレイトフル・デッド（1965年にカリフォルニア州サンフランシスコで結成されたロックバンド）　　☐ neuroscience 神経科学　　☐ Alzheimer's disease アルツハイマー病

TRUE OR FALSE?

1) ～ 5) のなかからニュースの内容として正しいものにはT、間違っているものにはFを選びなさい。

1) Contact with rhythm may help to improve brain function in people with neurological diseases.
2) Timing appears to have a big influence on the functioning of the brain.
3) Mickey Hart has just formed a rock group called The Grateful Dead.
4) Mickey Hart's grandmother suffered from Alzheimer's disease.
5) Mickey Hart says that playing the drums had a beneficial effect on his grandmother.

VOCABULARY BUILDING

下の語群の語を本文中で探して下線を引きなさい。そして、下の1) ～ 8) の英文の意味が通るように品詞・形などを変えたものを入れなさい。

1) To _____ a healthy life, it is important to eat and exercise well.
2) Teachers play a _____ role in children's development.
3) Chemists conduct _____ to determine the properties of various substances.
4) People with different _____ study English in different ways.
5) Do you know how to _____ this machinery?
6) I'm _____ in learning English through songs and movies.
7) People _____ from Alzheimer's disease may sleep at unusual times or refuse to eat.
8) This software has many useful _____.

| experiments | function | goal | interested |
| lead | major | operate | suffering |

USEFUL EXPRESSIONS

日本語に合うように（　　　）を埋めなさい。

1) 石けんあるいは合成洗剤との長期間の接触は皮膚病の原因となる可能性がある。

   Prolonged (　　　) with soap or detergent can lead to skin diseases.

2) 家に本があることは子どもの将来の学問的成功に大きな影響を与えるようだ。

   The presence of books in a home appears to have a major (　　　) on children's future academic success.

3) 建築家たちは耐震建物を設計するために伝統的な知識と現代科学を融合している。

   Architects are (　　　) traditional knowledge with modern science to design earthquake-resistant building.

4) あなたが私たちの会社に働きに来ることに興味があると聞いて私たちはとてもうれしい。

   We are very pleased to hear that you are (　　　) in coming to work for our company.

TRANSLATIONS

日本語に合うように（　　　）の語句を並び替えて、一文を完成させなさい。

1) アメリカの歴史では、数人の元将官が大統領にまで昇りつめている。

   In U.S. history, (become / former / generals / gone / have / on / president / several / to).

2) 糖尿病とエイズは世界の死亡原因のトップ10内に入る二つの病気である。

   Diabetes and AIDS (among / are / are / causes / death / diseases / in / of / that / the top / the world / two / 10).

6 | Farmed Christmas Trees: Good for the Environment?

クリスマスツリーは自然の木が良い？

VOCABULARY

(a) ～ (e) のなかから語義としてふさわしいものをそれぞれ選びなさい。

1) estimate   2) artificial   3) seedling

4) oxygen   5) storm

(a) to calculate approximately

(b) made by humans

(c) an occurrence of bad weather, often with rain and wind

(d) a gas necessary for life

(e) a young plant

1st Listening ▶▶▶ まず VOA ニュースを聴きましょう。

SUMMARY CHECK

ニュースの概要として最もふさわしいものを下の 1) ～ 4) のなかから選びなさい。

1) The National Christmas Tree Association was formed in 2012 to represent 10.9 million growers and sellers.

2) Cutting down Christmas trees is bad for the environment because it releases carbon dioxide into the atmosphere.

3) The National Christmas Tree Association says that natural Christmas trees are better for the environment than artificial trees.

4) Artificial trees from China last for an average of 6 to 9 years.

2nd Listening

▶▶▶ もう一回 VOA ニュースを聴き、(　　　) を埋めましょう。

From VOA Learning English, this is the Agriculture Report.

Americans love Christmas trees. The National Christmas Tree Association says more than 35 million of them were (1.　　　) in the United States in 2012. In large cities, many people buy trees that have already (2.　　　) cut. But some people (3.　　　) to a tree farm and cut their own tree.

The National Christmas Tree Association (4.　　　) growers and (5.　　　) of most of the farm-grown Christmas trees in the United States. It estimates that 10.9 million artificial trees were (6.　　　) in 2012, compared to 24.5 million (7.　　　) trees. The group says the (8.　　　) cost of a natural tree was $40. The (9.　　　) of an artificial one was about $70.

Most Christmas trees are now (10.　　　) on farms. The trees take 6 to 10 years to grow. To make sure there is always a (11.　　　), farmers usually plant 1 to 3 seedlings for every tree they cut down.

The Christmas tree association says real trees are better for the (12.　　　). That is because as Christmas trees grow, they (13.　　　) carbon dioxide and other gases while (14.　　　) fresh oxygen. The trees also help to protect water (15.　　　). Christmas trees are grown on soil that does not (16.　　　) other crops. After they are used, they can be cut up and used as fertilizer.

Christmas trees helped many East Coast communities after super-storm Sandy (17.　　　) the area. The trees were (18.　　　) near large hills of sandy soil to prevent erosion.

Artificial trees come mostly from China. They can be used year after year. They are usually made from plastic. Americans use them for an average of 6 to 9 years before (19.　　　) them away. But these trees can (20.　　　) in a landfill for hundreds of years.

For VOA Learning English, I'm Carolyn Presutti.

Notes
☐ National Christmas Tree Association 全米クリスマス・ツリー協会
☐ fertilizer 肥料   ☐ erosion 浸食   ☐ landfill 埋立地

TRUE OR FALSE?

1) ～ 5) のなかからニュースの内容として正しいものにはT、間違っているものにはFを選びなさい。

1) Fewer than 25,000,000 Christmas trees were sold in the United States in 2012, according to the National Christmas Tree Association.

2) In the U.S., some people buy trees that have been cut, some go to a tree farm to cut their own tree, and some buy artificial trees.

3) More artificial trees than natural trees were sold in the U.S. in 2012.

4) According to the National Christmas Tree Association, artificial trees are better for the environment.

5) Most artificial Christmas trees come from China.

VOCABULARY BUILDING

下の語群の語を本文中で探して下線を引きなさい。そして、下の1) ～ 8) の英文の意味が通るように品詞・形などを変えたものを入れなさい。

1) It is _____ that China's population is nearly 20% of the world's population.

2) Food prices in Japan are very high _____ to those in the USA.

3) When _____ are limited, prices tend to rise.

4) Forests _____ us with wood for building and many plants.

5) _____ accounts for about 20% of the Earth's atmosphere.

6) Many processed foods contain _____ additives.

7) _____ and Easter are two of the most important events in the Christian calendar.

8) A balanced diet can _____ you from heart disease.

| artificial | Christmas | compared | estimates |
| oxygen | protect | providing | supply |

USEFUL EXPRESSIONS

日本語に合うように（　　　）を埋めなさい。

1) アメリカでは、女性がすべてのビジネススクール卒業者に占める割合は、1970年の10%未満と比べて、2001年には半分だった。

   In the U.S., women constituted half of all business graduates in 2001, (　　　) to less than 10% in 1970.

2) 新入生が大学生活に慣れるのに1、2か月かかるのが普通だ。

   Freshmen usually (　　　) a month or two to get used to college life.

3) ソフトドリンクよりも健康に良いので、水か紅茶に切り替えることをお勧めします。

   I recommend switching to water or tea because they are (　　　) for your health than soft drinks.

4) 毎日長時間働くのは健康に悪影響を与える可能性がある。

   Working long hours day (　　　) day can have a bad effect on your health.

TRANSLATIONS

日本語に合うように（　　　）の語句を並び替えて、一文を完成させなさい。

1) 今日私たちが食べている非常に多くの食べ物にはその影響が不明瞭な幅広い人工添加物が含まれている。

   So many of the foods (of / we / artificial additives / contain / unclear / eat nowadays / whose / a wide / effects / are / range).

   ....

2) 世界中の約300万人が毎年喫煙が関係する病気で亡くなると推定されている。

   It (about / die / estimated / every year / from / is / people worldwide / smoking-related / that / 3,000,000) diseases.

   ....

7 Can Mothers' Milk Beat HIV?

タンパク質が HIV から赤ん坊を救う？

VOCABULARY

(a) ～ (e) のなかから語義としてふさわしいものをそれぞれ選びなさい。

1) virus   2) pregnancy   3) suppress

4) protein   5) harmless

(a) a substance found in meat, eggs, etc.

(b) a very small organism that can cause a disease

(c) a period of time before birth

(d) something that does not cause damage

(e) to stop or reduce something

1st Listening ▶▶▶ まず VOA ニュースを聴きましょう。

SUMMARY CHECK

ニュースの概要として最もふさわしいものを下の 1) ～ 4) のなかから選びなさい。

1) Sallie Permar suggests that TNC should be called by its full name, Tenacin-C.

2) Breastfeeding should be avoided by most mothers, in case of HIV infection.

3) Scientists have identified a protein in breast milk that suppresses HIV.

4) Scientists fear that the number of children infected with the AIDS virus each year may reach the hundreds of thousands.

[25]

2nd Listening

▶▶▶ もう一回 VOA ニュースを聴き、(　　　) を埋めましょう。

From VOA Learning English, this is the Health Report.

Hundreds of (1.　　　) of children become infected with the AIDS virus every year. These boys and girls are (2.　　　) to mothers who have HIV—the human immunodeficiency virus. The children become infected during pregnancy or from (3.　　　).

Recently, scientists (4.　　　) a protein in breast milk that suppresses the virus. Now, experts say the (5.　　　) could lead to new ways to protect babies (6.　　　) mothers are infected with HIV.

Doctors have (7.　　　) the number of infections by giving antiretroviral drugs to both mothers and their babies. But experts say that even without anti-AIDS drugs, only a small (8.　　　) of babies become infected (9.　　　) breast milk.

Sallie Permar is a professor of pediatrics and immunology at Duke University in North Carolina. She says infected women who breastfeed can expose babies to the virus (10.　　　). Yet only 10 percent of those babies will become infected. Professor Permar (11.　　　) an effort to identify a substance in breast milk that may (12.　　　) babies from infection. Her (13.　　　) studied a protein called Tenacin-C, also called TNC. It is known to be involved in the process of (14.　　　) wounds.

The researchers exposed the TNC protein from breast milk of (15.　　　) women to HIV. The protein (16.　　　) up to the virus and made it (17.　　　). Professor Permar and her team suggest that TNC could be used where costly drug treatments are not (18.　　　). She suggests that this (19.　　　) part of human milk could be given to babies before breastfeeding to provide more (20.　　　).

The team reported its findings in the journal *Proceedings of the National Academy of Sciences*.

For VOA Learning English, I'm Laurel Bowman.

Notes

- □ human immunodeficiency virus(= HIV) ヒト免疫不全ウイルス、エイズウイルス
- □ antiretroviral drug 抗レトロウイルス薬　　□ pediatrics 小児科
- □ immunology 免疫学　　□ Duke University デューク大学
- □ *Proceedings of the National Academy of Sciences*『米国科学アカデミー紀要』

TRUE OR FALSE?

1)～5) のなかからニュースの内容として正しいものにはT、間違っているものにはFを選びなさい。

1) It is not possible for children to be infected with HIV during pregnancy.

2) Antiretroviral drugs cannot be given to babies.

3) Most babies exposed to the HIV virus through breastfeeding will be infected with AIDS.

4) Tenacin-C is involved in healing wounds and may also make the HIV virus harmless.

5) Tenacin-C may be useful in places where other treatments are too expensive.

VOCABULARY BUILDING

下の語群の語を本文中で探して下線を引きなさい。そして、下の1)～8)の英文の意味が通るように品詞・形などを変えたものを入れなさい。

1) A virus can _____ your computer via email or a USB stick.

2) The _____ of electricity played a major part in the development of civilisation.

3) The police weren't able to _____ the criminal.

4) To slow global warming, it is important to _____ the use of fossil fuels.

5) Aspartame is a _____ that is used to sweeten food.

6) Many drugs are best avoided during _____.

7) Young people need lots of _____ in order to grow and remain healthy.

8) A delay in making an important decision can be very _____.

| costly | discovery | identified | infected |
| pregnancy | protein | reduced | substance |

USEFUL EXPRESSIONS

日本語に合うように（　　　）を埋めなさい。

1) 寒い冬の時期にはインフルエンザにかかりやすい。

   It is very easy to become (　　　　) with the flu during the cold winter days.

2) 学生時代にはさまざまな経験に身をさらすことが大切だ。

   It is important during your time at college to (　　　　) yourself to a wide range of experiences.

3) エイズが初めて現れたときにはよく分からないことだったが、今ではヒト免疫不全ウイルスが原因だと知られている。

   AIDS was a big mystery when it first appeared, but it is now (　　　　) to be caused by the human immunodeficiency virus.

4) 科学者たちは老化を遅らせるのに関わる酵素を発見した。

   Scientists have found an enzyme that is (　　　　) in slowing aging.

TRANSLATIONS

日本語に合うように（　　　）の語句を並び替えて、一文を完成させなさい。

1) イルカやクジラのいくつかの種の妊娠期間は 19 か月にも及ぶことがある。

   The duration of (as / be / can / dolphin and whale / in / long as / of / pregnancies / some species) 19 months.

   ....

2) 臨床試験で患者にプラシーボ（偽薬）を与えることはある意味では不誠実だが、多くの恩恵をもたらす可能性のある安全な行為であると見なされている。

   Giving patients a placebo in a medical trial is in a sense dishonest but (a harmless practice / as / being / bring / can / is / it / many benefits / recognized / that).

   ....

8 | The World's Largest Solar Power Plant

太陽エネルギーの有効利用

VOCABULARY

(a) ～ (e) のなかから語義としてふさわしいものをそれぞれ選びなさい。

1) thermal   2) harm   3) mirror
4) temperature   5) electricity

(a) a surface that reflects images

(b) to do damage to something

(c) a kind of energy that is used to power lights, machines, and so on

(d) related to heat

(e) a measure of heat

 1st Listening ▶▶▶ まず VOA ニュースを聴きましょう。

SUMMARY CHECK

ニュースの概要として最もふさわしいものを下の 1) ～ 4) のなかから選びなさい。

1) Joe Desmond and Lisa Belenky are hoping to merge BrightSource Energy and the Center for Biological Diversity.

2) Joe Desmond is opposed to heating steam to temperatures above 260℃.

3) The Mojave Desert is the only place in the U.S. where solar power plants are allowed.

4) Although solar power is generally considered clean, environmentalists are worried about the environmental impact of the very large Ivanpah plant in the Mojave Desert.

2nd Listening

▶▶▶ もう一回 VOA ニュースを聴き、(　　　) を埋めましょう。

From VOA Learning English, this is the Technology Report.

The world's largest solar thermal (1.　　　) was set to begin producing power in the United States at the end of 2013. Wind and energy from the sun are generally (2.　　　) clean, (3.　　　) energy from coal-burning power stations. But, environmentalists now (4.　　　) that too much solar power (5.　　　) could harm the environment.

A California company, BrightSource Energy, has been building a (6.　　　) solar power plant in the Mojave Desert, about 60 kilometers southwest of Las Vegas, Nevada. The plant is called the Ivanpah Solar Electric Generating System. The company (7.　　　) to deploy 170,000 specially (8.　　　) mirrors to direct solar energy towards boilers on top of three towers. The steam produced in the boilers will (9.　　　) turbines to make electricity.

Joe Desmond works for BrightSource Energy. He says the steam can reach temperatures of more than 260 (10.　　　) Celsius. He says the plant can (11.　　　) the sun's thermal energy in the form of molten salt. With stored energy, he says, the power station can produce electricity even when the sun goes (12.　　　).

Environmentalists generally (13.　　　) the idea of solar power. But there are (14.　　　). Lisa Belenky is with a (15.　　　) group called the Center for Biological Diversity. She says environmentalists are (16.　　　) about the effect of the Ivanpah Solar Project on the sensitive plant and animal life in the Mojave Desert. That (17.　　　) birds striking solar equipment or being (18.　　　) after flying through the intense heat. As solar projects (19.　　　), developers and environmentalists are considering what to do to (20.　　　) bird deaths.

For VOA Learning English, I'm Carolyn Presutti.

Notes

- Mojave Desert モハーベ砂漠（カリフォルニア州南部にある砂漠）
- Ivanpah Solar Electric Generating System イヴァンパー・ソーラー・エレクトリック・ジェネレーティング・システム（世界最大のソーラー発電所）　☐ deploy 配備する　☐ molten salt 溶融塩
- Center for Biological Diversity 生物多様性センター　☐ sensitive 敏感な

TRUE OR FALSE?

1) ～ 5) のなかからニュースの内容として正しいものには T、間違っているものには F を選びなさい。

1)　Solar power is generally considered clean.

2)　The Ivanpah Solar Electric Generating System is located in California.

3)　The plant can produce steam of up to 260°C.

4)　Lisa Belenky works for a governmental group.

5)　Environmentalists are worried about birds being burned.

VOCABULARY BUILDING

下の語群の語を本文中で探して下線を引きなさい。そして、下の 1) ～ 8) の英文の意味が通るように品詞・形などを変えたものを入れなさい。

1)　Smoking and drinking alcohol can _____ your health.

2)　Solar, wave, and wind power are considered to be _____ than energy from fossil fuels.

3)　The supermarket decided to _____ remote-controlled cameras to spot criminal activity.

4)　A good way to heat a large building is to generate steam in a _____ and circulate it round the building through pipes.

5)　These days, there are many _____ about food safety.

6)　Champagne is a kind of sparkling wine _____ in the Champagne region of France.

7)　Water boils at a _____ of 100°C.

8)　The new bypass will _____ traveling time by about half.

| boilers | clean | concerns | deploy |
| harm | produce | reduce | temperature |

USEFUL EXPRESSIONS

日本語に合うように（　　　）を埋めなさい。

1) あの選手は地元のチームから世界でトップのチームの一つに移ることになっている。

   The player is (　　　) to leave his local team for one of the top teams in the world.

2) オックスフォードはイギリスのロンドン中心部から北西約 60 マイルのところに位置する有名な学園都市です。

   Oxford is a famous university town located about 60 miles northwest (　　　) central London in the UK.

3) 環境に優しい設計は環境に対する超高層ビルの影響が最低限になるであろうことを意味する。

   Its eco-friendly design means that the effects of the skyscraper (　　　) the environment will be minimal.

4) 医療緊急事態では、救急車が到着するまでに患者を助けるためにどうすべきかを学ぶことが重要だ。

   In medical emergencies, it is important to learn (　　　) to do to help the patient until the ambulance arrives.

TRANSLATIONS

日本語に合うように（　　　）の語句を並び替えて、一文を完成させなさい。

1) 電気の豊富な供給がない高度な文明を想像するのは難しい。

   It (advanced / civilization / difficult / electricity / imagine / is / of / plentiful / supplies / to / without).

   ....

2) 太陽の中心部の温度は 2,500 万度に達すると言われている。

   The (core / is / of / reach / said / Sun's / temperature / the / to) 25,000,000 degrees.

   ....

9 | Is Community-Based Mental Health Treatment Better?

統合失調症には在宅治療が効果的？

VOCABULARY

(a) ～ (e) のなかから語義としてふさわしいものをそれぞれ選びなさい。

1) disabling 2) reality 3) seek
4) medication 5) patient

(a) drugs given to someone to treat an illness

(b) causing someone to be unable to work or do daily activities as before

(c) to look for

(d) what actually happens rather than what is imagined

(e) someone who is sick and receiving medical treatment

1st Listening ▶▶▶ まず VOA ニュースを聴きましょう。

SUMMARY CHECK

ニュースの概要として最もふさわしいものを下の 1) ～ 4) のなかから選びなさい。

1) A study shows that community care is beneficial in schizophrenia treatment.

2) Graham Thornicroft leads most of the schizophrenia studies conducted at the Institute of Psychiatry at Kings College.

3) 95% of patients treated at Kings College improve within one year.

4) Studies involving nearly 300 patients with schizophrenia will soon begin in India.

2nd Listening

▶▶▶ もう一回 VOA ニュースを聴き、(　　　) を埋めましょう。

From VOA Learning English, this is the Health Report.

Schizophrenia is a long-term and often disabling (1.　　　) disorder. People with schizophrenia suffer a (2.　　　) in the links among their thoughts, feelings and behavior. They may hear (3.　　　) that other people do not.

Schizophrenics often withdraw from (4.　　　)—from family and friends. This (5.　　　) they may not seek help for the disorder. The main (6.　　　) for schizophrenia is medication. But sufferers may forget to take their (7.　　　). Now, research suggests that community-based, in-home care is an (8.　　　) method for treating people with schizophrenia.

The study involved almost 300 schizophrenic patients in India. All the patients were between 16 and 60 years old. Researchers looked at community care for these men and women in their homes. Then the researchers (9.　　　) it to the care (10.　　　) at mental health centers.

Study leader Graham Thornicroft is with the Institute of Psychiatry at Kings College in London. He says health care workers (11.　　　) the homes of 187 schizophrenic patients. The workers gave the patients medication and follow-up care (12.　　　) doctor visits. They (13.　　　) family members how to care for their (14.　　　) ones. The in-home care was (15.　　　) with visits to mental health centers.

The (16.　　　) of this group was compared to 95 patients who received care only at mental health centers. Mr. Thornicroft says that a year later the patients who received in-home care showed major (17.　　　). He said they were more (18.　　　) to the real world, had (19.　　　) problems and were more (20.　　　) to take their medicine.

For VOA Learning English, I'm Alex Villarreal.

Notes
☐ schizophrenia 統合失調症　☐ withdraw from~ 〜から引きこもる
☐ Institute of Psychiatry 精神医学研究所　☐ King's College (ロンドン大学) キングズカレッジ

TRUE OR FALSE?

1) 〜 5) のなかからニュースの内容として正しいものには T、間違っているものには F を選びなさい。

1) Some people with schizophrenia hear voices that other people do not.

2) Some schizophrenics do not seek help.

3) The study described was carried out in London.

4) In the study, some patients were given follow-up visits between visits to mental health centers, and others were not.

5) There appeared to be no difference between the two groups of patients.

VOCABULARY BUILDING

下の語群の語を本文中で探して下線を引きなさい。そして、下の 1) 〜 8) の英文の意味が通るように品詞・形などを変えたものを入れなさい。

1) He is _____ from a bad cold so he won't be joining us today.

2) Before going abroad it is good to learn what kinds of _____ are considered unacceptable.

3) The athlete was injured so he _____ from the competition.

4) The best _____ for a cold is probably rest and drinking plenty of hot drinks.

5) Dentists say that fluoride is _____ against cavities.

6) The _____ between drug use and crime is clear.

7) When going on a trip, don't forget to take any prescription _____.

8) He _____ all about their wedding anniversary.

| behavior | effective | forget | link |
| medication | suffer | treatment | withdraw |

USEFUL EXPRESSIONS

日本語に合うように（　　　）を埋めなさい。

1) 緑茶と運動を組み合わせると人が体重を減らすのを促すと最近の研究は示唆する。

   Recent research (　　　) that green tea and exercise together can help people lose weight.

2) 塩素化は飲料水を消毒するのに費用のかからない効果的な方法だ。

   Chlorination is an inexpensive and effective (　　　) for disinfecting drinking water.

3) 数千人が関わった研究が、アスピリンが心臓発作と脳卒中のリスクを減らす可能性があることを示している。

   Studies (　　　) thousands of people have shown that aspirin can reduce the risk of heart attack and stroke.

4) 最近の研究によると、女性のCEO（最高経営責任者）は男性のCEOよりも解雇される確率が高い。

   According to recent research, female CEOs are more (　　　) to be fired than male CEOs.

TRANSLATIONS

日本語に合うように（　　　）の語句を並び替えて、一文を完成させなさい。

1) 薬を服用するのを忘れたり、正しく服用しなかったりすることは深刻な医療上の問題となると医学の専門家は警告する。

   Medical experts (a / correctly / failing to / forgetting to / is / major / medical problem / or / take medications / take them / that / warn).

   ....

2) より効果的な治療法は、病院がそれだけ早く患者を退院させることが可能になり、必要性がより差し迫った人たちにベッドが利用できるようにする。

   More effective medical treatments can (and make / available / beds / discharge patients / enable / for / hospitals / more / need is / sooner / those whose / to) urgent.

   ....

10 How Can Farmers Use Social Media?

農業とソーシャルメディア

VOCABULARY

(a) 〜 (e) のなかから語義としてふさわしいものをそれぞれ選びなさい。

1) waste　　　2) agriculture　　　3) profit

4) employee　　5) deal

(a) an offer at a reduced price

(b) a monetary or financial gain

(c) to consume something uselessly

(d) the practice of farming

(e) someone who works for another person for a salary

1st Listening ▶▶▶ まず VOA ニュースを聴きましょう。

SUMMARY CHECK

ニュースの概要として最もふさわしいものを下の 1) 〜 4) のなかから選びなさい。

1) Most food these days is sold through Facebook.

2) The United Nations decided to hold World Environment Day in June from next year.

3) Bloomfield Farms in Sonoma County is using social media to help reduce food wastage.

4) Bloomfield Farms produces top-quality greens and carrots throughout the year.

2nd Listening
▶▶▶ もう一回 VOA ニュースを聴き、(　　　) を埋めましょう。

From VOA Learning English, this is the Agriculture Report.

On World Environment Day in June, the United Nations reported that at least one third of all food produced is (1.　　　). The report came at a time when many people are concerned about how to (2.　　　) a growing world population.

In the United States, farmers who are (3.　　　) to earn money find the situation difficult to deal with. The United States Department of Agriculture found that more than (4.　　　) of the small farms in California do not make a profit.

One California farm family is using social (5.　　　) in an effort to change the situation and (6.　　　) wasted food. Nick Papadopoulos is general (7.　　　) of Bloomfield Farms in Sonoma County. It was difficult for him to watch his employees (8.　　　) from several weekend farmers' markets with top quality, (9.　　　) produce. Mr. Papadopoulos said he would find boxes of leafy greens, herbs and carrots (10.　　　) in a storage area. The vegetables would go (11.　　　) before the next market day.

As a (12.　　　), Mr. Papadopoulos came up with a plan to (13.　　　) the food at a low price by (14.　　　) it on the farmer's Facebook status page on Sunday nights. The (15.　　　) were open to anyone using the social media website. One week, several homeowners in a (16.　　　) community bought the vegetables. Another week, the (17.　　　) were a group of friends.

Nick Papadopoulos began using social media after he went to work on a farm (18.　　　) to his wife's father. After his (19.　　　) of using Facebook, Mr. Papadopoulos helped to set up a website called cropmobster.com. It is a place where people involved with food production can find (20.　　　) food for many causes.

For VOA Learning English, I'm Alex Villarreal.

Notes
☐ World Environment Day 世界環境デー　　☐ United Nations 国際連合
☐ United States Department of Agriculture 米国農務省　　☐ Sonoma County ソノマ郡（カリフォルニア州サンフランシスコの北約 55 キロメートルに位置する郡）

TRUE OR FALSE?

1) 〜 5) のなかからニュースの内容として正しいものには T、間違っているものには F を選びなさい。

1) A United Nations report says that less than one third of food produced is eaten.

2) Nearly all small farms in California make a profit.

3) Nick Papadopoulos's employees were very kind and would always buy herbs and vegetables for him at the market.

4) Mr. Papadopoulos found that selling food cheaply on Facebook on Sunday nights was a good way to reduce wasted food.

5) Cropmobster.com is a website where it is possible to find surplus food.

VOCABULARY BUILDING

下の語群の語を本文中で探して下線を引きなさい。そして、下の 1) 〜 8) の英文の意味が通るように品詞・形などを変えたものを入れなさい。

1) It is important to teach children not to _____ food.

2) More and more people are _____ about extreme weather events.

3) These days, many people _____ to achieve work–life balance.

4) Higher education _____ the people of developing nations a great opportunity to improve their economic circumstances.

5) Many people _____ with the movie business gather at the annual film festival.

6) My father worked on a dairy _____ his whole life.

7) Nurses in most countries don't _____ very much.

8) It takes a lot of time and _____ to write a graduation thesis.

| concerned | earn | effort | farm |
| involved | offer | struggling | wasted |

USEFUL EXPRESSIONS

日本語に合うように（　　　）を埋めなさい。

1) 世界の農産物の少なくとも3分の1は受粉のためにハチやその他の昆虫に依存する。

   At (　　　) one third of the world's agricultural crops depend on bees and other insects for pollination.

2) 地球温暖化は対応するのがとても難しいさまざまな問題を引き起こしている。

   Global warming is causing all kinds of problems that are very difficult to deal (　　　).

3) 私たちはこの問題の解決法を迅速に考え出す必要がある。

   We need to (　　　) up with a solution to this problem in short order.

4) この科目は十分なGPA（成績評価値）を持つ誰もが参加できる。

   This course is (　　　) to anyone with an adequate Grade Point Average.

TRANSLATIONS

日本語に合うように（　　　）の語句を並び替えて、一文を完成させなさい。

1) 農業はアメリカの国内総生産のわずか1％にしかすぎない。

   Agriculture (about / accounts / for / GDP / in / of / only / the / 1%) U.S.

   ....

2) 無駄になる食べ物の量を減らそうと様々な手段が提案されている。賞味期限を調整したり、ソーシャルメディア・サイトで食べ物を販売することである。

   Various (been / food / have / measures / of / suggested / the amount / to reduce / to try / wasted), including adjusting sell-by dates and selling food on social media sites.

   ....

11 How Can We Get Children to Eat Better?

いかに子供たちの食料供給を増やすか

VOCABULARY

(a) ～ (e) のなかから語義としてふさわしいものをそれぞれ選びなさい。

1) education   2) dairy   3) underfeeding

4) measure   5) confirm

(a) milk and foods made from milk

(b) to find the amount or quantity of something

(c) to decide whether something is really true

(d) learning or teaching in a systematic way

(e) being given not enough food

 1st Listening ▶▶▶ まず VOA ニュースを聴きましょう。

SUMMARY CHECK

ニュースの概要として最もふさわしいものを下の 1) ～ 4) のなかから選びなさい。

1) Mahila Samakhya is one of many groups in southern India.

2) Kathy Baylis is an economist.

3) A study has shown that Indian children eat better when their mothers have more power and education.

4) It is important for children to eat as much dairy food as possible.

2nd Listening

▶▶▶ もう一回 VOA ニュースを聴き、(　　　) を埋めましょう。

From VOA Learning English, this is the Health Report.

New research in India shows that children eat (1.　　　) when their mothers have more power, more education and are able to move about (2.　　　) in their communities. Researchers found that women who (3.　　　) a job skills training program (4.　　　) more in control at home and in their families. And the children of these women (5.　　　) more rice and dairy foods.

A program in southern India is (6.　　　) Mahila Samakhya. It brings women together to form (7.　　　) support groups. Researchers at the University of Illinois questioned if and how these groups (8.　　　) the women's sense of themselves and their (9.　　　) in the family.

Kathy Baylis is an economist at the College of Agricultural, Consumer and Environmental Sciences at the University of Illinois. She (10.　　　) the study. Ms Baylis says that before (11.　　　) the peer groups, the women knew (12.　　　) than five other women to whom they were not (13.　　　). Ms. Baylis (14.　　　) that many of them did not know the (15.　　　) for women in work and in family life.

Experts say 40 percent of Indian children under the age of five suffer from underfeeding. But Ms. Baylis says (16.　　　) in the support groups led them to provide better foods for their children. Researchers visited the homes of those (17.　　　) in the groups. They created a simple measuring process. They (18.　　　) different sized food bowls and asked the mothers (19.　　　) size bowls they were using. Researchers confirmed that the children were eating better based on the size of bowl the mothers used. They found that girls (20.　　　) started eating more.

For VOA Learning English, I'm Laurel Bowman.

Notes
- University of Illinois イリノイ大学
- College of Agricultural, Consumer and Environmental Sciences 農業・消費・環境科学学部
- peer group 仲間集団
- confirm 確認する

TRUE OR FALSE?

1) 〜 5) のなかからニュースの内容として正しいものには T、間違っているものには F を選びなさい。

1) Kathy Baylis's study found that a job skills training program helped women feel more in control at home.

2) Mahila Samakhya is a program that brings University of Illinois students together.

3) Kathy Baylis is a psychologist.

4) It is said that more than half of Indian children under the age of five suffer from underfeeding.

5) Involvement in support groups caused mothers to provide better foods for their children.

VOCABULARY BUILDING

下の語群の語を本文中で探して下線を引きなさい。そして、下の 1) 〜 8) の英文の意味が通るように品詞・形などを変えたものを入れなさい。

1) Improving your English will enable you to converse _____ with people from many countries.

2) _____-based healthcare often works better than healthcare in large, faraway hospitals.

3) Many companies have found that workers are often happier when they are in _____ of their own schedules.

4) _____ products are a key part of the diet in most European nations.

5) The weather can _____ our moods in positive and negative ways.

6) It is important that new factories should benefit _____ residents.

7) His experiences led him to _____ his beliefs.

8) He lay in a comfortable _____, daydreaming.

| affected | communities | control | dairy |
| freely | local | position | question |

USEFUL EXPRESSIONS

日本語に合うように（　　　）を埋めなさい。

1) 自分の環境を管理していると感じることは寿命を延ばす可能性があることが、ある研究で分かった。

   A study has found that feeling in (　　　) of one's circumstances can prolong life.

2) 日本人の約3人に1人が花粉症に苦しむと推測されている。

   It has been estimated that about one in three Japanese (　　　) from pollen allergies.

3) 過去を忘れた人はそれ（過去）を繰り返すよう運命づけられている。

   (　　　) who forget the past are condemned to repeat it.

4) 今日の上映の観客の反応に基づいて、この映画はとても評判がよくなると思う。

   I think this movie is going to be very popular, (　　　) on the reaction of the audience at today's showing.

TRANSLATIONS

日本語に合うように（　　　）の語句を並び替えて、一文を完成させなさい。

1) 教育は国の発展に唯一最大の要素であると研究者は言う。

   Researchers say that (a / country / development / education / factor / important / in / is / most / of / the / the single).

   ....

2) 最近の研究によると、小児期の栄養のある朝食は、学校でのより良い成績へとつながり、成人の肥満の可能性を減らす。

   A recent study confirms that (a nutritious / achievement / adult / and / at / better / breakfast / childhood / during / leads / obesity / of / reduces / school / the likelihood / to).

   ....

12 | Making Agriculture Sustainable

農業による環境汚染を減らす方法

VOCABULARY

(a) ～ (e) のなかから語義としてふさわしいものをそれぞれ選びなさい。

1) hurt   2) fertilizer   3) transportation

4) drought   5) urban

(a) related to towns or cities

(b) to damage something

(c) moving people or things from one place to another

(d) a substance used to make plants grow better

(e) a time when very little rain falls

 1st Listening ▶▶▶ まず VOA ニュースを聴きましょう。

SUMMARY CHECK

ニュースの概要として最もふさわしいものを下の 1) ～ 4) のなかから選びなさい。

1) Danielle Nierenberg is the author of several Worldwatch Institute reports.

2) A Worldwatch Institute report suggests some ways in which agriculture can reduce its impact on the environment.

3) Growing more food in cities can reduce transportation costs.

4) There has recently been an 88% decrease in carbon dioxide in the atmosphere.

[45]

2nd Listening

▶▶▶ もう一回 VOA ニュースを聴き、(　　　) を埋めましょう。

From VOA Learning English, this is the Agriculture Report.

Agriculture produces a lot of the heat-trapping gases that scientists link to (1.　　　) temperatures and climate change. Agriculture also can be hurt by the effects of climate change.

The Worldwatch Institute in Washington (2.　　　) ways that agriculture can reduce its effects on the environment. Worldwatch (3.　　　) a report called *Innovations in Sustainable Agriculture: Supporting Climate-Friendly Food Production.*

Researcher Danielle Nierenberg was one of its (4.　　　). She says 25 to 30 percent of all (5.　　　) gas emissions come from agriculture. This is (6.　　　) fertilizers, pesticides, antibiotic drugs, transportation and processing are all dependent on oil, gas and (7.　　　). Danielle Nierenberg says animal (8.　　　) has an especially big effect on the environment. She notes that more meat is being (9.　　　) in countries like Brazil, China and India. As a result, more (10.　　　) factory farms are being built in the (11.　　　) world.

The report (12.　　　) six land and water use practices that it says are sustainable. These (13.　　　) growing trees on farmland to reduce soil erosion and planting cover crops to (14.　　　) soil from drought, heat and pests. Danielle Nierenberg says urban (15.　　　) can help as well. Growing more food in cities can reduce transportation (16.　　　), she says. Urban (17.　　　) then can buy food from within their communities.

Other recommendations include (18.　　　) waste water in cities, drip irrigation, and catching and (19.　　　) rainwater. The United Nations (20.　　　) that changes in the agriculture industry could cut its carbon dioxide production by 88 percent.

For VOA Learning English, I'm Alex Villareal.

Notes

☐ Worldwatch Institute ワールドウォッチ研究所（地球環境問題に取り組むことを目的に設立された組織）　☐ *Innovations in Sustainable Agriculture: Supporting Climate-Friendly Food Production*『持続可能な農業の革命：気候に優しい食料生産の支援』　☐ emission 放出　☐ pesticide 殺虫剤　☐ antibiotic drug 抗生物質　☐ transportation 運送　☐ drought 干ばつ　☐ drip irrigation 点滴灌漑

TRUE OR FALSE?

1) ～5) のなかからニュースの内容として正しいものにはT、間違っているものにはFを選びなさい。

1) Agriculture is affected by climate change.
2) A lot of greenhouse gas emissions come from agriculture.
3) Animal production has a very big effect on the environment.
4) Growing trees on farmland is bad for the environment.
5) Danielle Nierenberg advises against urban farming.

VOCABULARY BUILDING

下の語群の語を本文中で探して下線を引きなさい。そして、下の1)～8)の英文の意味が通るように品詞・形などを変えたものを入れなさい。

1) That factory _____ a wide range of goods.
2) The use of fossil fuels has been _____ to climate change.
3) The _____ of this drug are still unclear.
4) Japan's economy is _____ on exports.
5) The government hopes to bring _____ economic growth.
6) Solar panels _____ the sun's heat to use to warm the house or make electricity.
7) The best way to lose weight is to _____ your eating habits.
8) One promising _____ in farming is agricultural drones.

change	dependent	effects	innovations
link	produces	sustainable	trap

USEFUL EXPRESSIONS

日本語に合うように（　　　）を埋めなさい。

1) 科学者はマラリアに感染した病歴が学校の成績が低いことと関係していると言う。

   Scientists (　　　) a history of malaria infection to lower achievement in school.

2) 公共交通機関が不足しているため、多くの地方の人たちは自動車に頼っている。

   Because of the lack of public transportation, people in many rural areas are (　　　) on automobiles.

3) 大気汚染は多くの都市の生活の質に大きな影響を及ぼす。

   Air pollution has a huge (　　　) on the quality of life in many cities.

4) 欧州連合におけるアルコール消費量は世界で最も多いが、今では30年前よりも消費されるアルコールは減っている。

   Alcohol consumption in the European Union is the highest in the world but less alcohol is (　　　) consumed now than 30 years ago.

TRANSLATIONS

日本語に合うように（　　　）の語句を並び替えて、一文を完成させなさい。

1) 公共交通機関のシステムはより良い生活の質をもたらし、多くの環境問題の解決に役立つ可能性がある。

   Public transportation systems (a / and / better / bring / can / environmental / help / life / many / of / problems / quality / solve / to).

   ....

2) 地球温暖化は多くの国でますます頻繁に起きている洪水や干ばつの原因となっているようだ。

   Global warming (and / appears / be / causing / countries / droughts in / floods / frequent / increasingly / many / to).

   ....

13 Diet at the Root of Tooth Decay?

ダイエットは虫歯の原因になる？

VOCABULARY

(a) ～ (e) のなかから語義としてふさわしいものをそれぞれ選びなさい。

1) diet   2) oral   3) decay

4) continent   5) chew

(a) a large landmass

(b) to use the mouth to make food easier to digest

(c) related to the mouth

(d) a kind of damage

(e) the foods that people eat

1st Listening ▶▶▶ まず VOA ニュースを聴きましょう。

SUMMARY CHECK

ニュースの概要として最もふさわしいものを下の 1) ～ 4) のなかから選びなさい。

1) The Institute of Dentistry at the University of London is leading a team of researchers who are trying to estimate rates of infection from tooth decay around the world.

2) A report says that tooth decay is a serious and spreading health problem and calls for action to address the problem.

3) Professor Marcenes will become the leader of a dental research team in order to campaign for better dental health.

4) Fluoride should be added to water in sub-Saharan Africa.

2nd Listening

▶▶▶ もう一回 VOA ニュースを聴き、(　　　) を埋めましょう。

From VOA Learning English, this is the Health Report.

Nearly 4 (1.　　　) people around the world have (2.　　　), untreated problems with their teeth. That is what a (3.　　　) report from the World Health Organization says. Health officials say (4.　　　) to repair cavities can even lead to social and (5.　　　) problems.

Wagner Marcenes is with the Institute of Dentistry at Queen Mary, University of London. He led a team of researchers as (6.　　　) of the Global Burden of Disease 2010 study. They used the information to (7.　　　) rates of infection. The report says untreated tooth decay is the most (8.　　　) of all 291 major diseases and injuries.

Professor Marcenes says increases in tooth decay are (9.　　　) sub-Saharan Africa and probably other (10.　　　) on the continent. He says this increase in tooth decay could be a result of (11.　　　) in diet, as developing countries (12.　　　) western-style diets. Many western diets are rich in sugar, a (13.　　　) cause of health problems in the mouth. But, in western countries, water (14.　　　) are often treated with the chemical fluoride. Adding fluoride to the water makes teeth (15.　　　) to the bacteria that can cause tooth decay.

Wagner Marcenes says oral health problems can have a major effect on a person's (16.　　　) of life. Cavities make eating difficult. As a result, people may eat softer foods that are easier to chew. However, softer foods are often higher in (17.　　　).

Professor Marcenes is calling for an "urgent, organized, social (18.　　　)" to oral health problems. He believes in fighting tooth decay through a (19.　　　) diet. He is also calling for the development of new and less costly dental (20.　　　) and treatments.

For VOA Learning English, I'm Mario Ritter.

Notes
- cavity 虫歯
- Institute of Dentistry at Queen Mary, University of London ロンドン大学クイーン・メアリ歯科研究所
- Global Burden of Disease 2010 study (= GBD 2010) 世界の疾病負担研究 2010（正式には Global Burden Diseases, Injuries, and Risk Factors Study）
- sub-Saharan Africa サハラ砂漠以南のアフリカ諸国
- fluoride フッ化物

TRUE OR FALSE?

1) ～5) のなかからニュースの内容として正しいものには T、間違っているものには F を選びなさい。

1) The number of people worldwide who have serious, untreated problems with their teeth is about 400,000,000.

2) Wagner Marcenes took part in the Global Burden of Disease 2010 study.

3) Researchers found that untreated tooth decay was the tenth most common of 291 major diseases and injuries.

4) Increases in tooth decay in sub-Saharan Africa may be due to a shift towards western-style diets.

5) Wagner Marcenes says that less expensive dental treatments should be developed.

VOCABULARY BUILDING

下の語群の語を本文中で探して下線を引きなさい。そして、下の 1) ～ 8) の英文の意味が通るように品詞・形などを変えたものを入れなさい。

1) When _____, a disease often gets worse and worse.

2) _____ to hand in all your homework on time may lead to a low grade.

3) We _____ that it will take six months to finish this project.

4) I recommend that get your roof _____ before it rains again.

5) Problems in the economy can lead to an _____ in crime.

6) The current economic difficulties mean that all of us will have to assume a heavy _____.

7) The unemployment _____ has risen to more than 10%.

8) Doctors advise people against taking _____ in their coffee and tea.

| burden | estimate | failure | increases |
| rate | repair | sugar | untreated |

USEFUL EXPRESSIONS

日本語に合うように（　　　）を埋めなさい。

1) 宿題の締め切り前夜にコンピュータの調子が悪く、徹夜して宿題を終わらせなければならなかった。

   I had problems (　　　) my computer the evening before the assignment deadline and had to work through the night to finish it.

2) 日本では、平均寿命が1960年の約67歳から現在の約82歳に徐々に上昇している。

   In Japan, there has been a steady increase (　　　) life expectancy from about 67 years in 1960 to about 82 years now.

3) ペットを買うときには犬よりも猫の方が世話しやすいということを考えるべきだ。

   You should remember when buying a pet that cats are (　　　) to care for than dogs.

4) 多くの文明病は防ぐことができるので、医学の研究者はそれらと闘うための世界的な取り組みを呼びかけている。

   Since many diseases of civilization are preventable, medical researchers are (　　　) for a coordinated global effort to combat them.

TRANSLATIONS

日本語に合うように（　　　）の語句を並び替えて、一文を完成させなさい。

1) 工業先進国からアフリカへの口腔の疾病の広がりは多くの医師たちを心配させている。

   The (Africa / diseases / from / is / nations / of / oral / spread / the industrialized / to / worrying) many doctors.

   ....

2) 1970年代から、都市の衰退は北米とヨーロッパの地域の多くの都市で主要な問題となっている。

   Since the 1970s, (a / been / cities / decay / has / in / in / major / many / problem / urban) North America and parts of Europe.

   ....

14 Concerns about Ethanol

エタノールとトウモロコシの意外な関係

VOCABULARY

(a) 〜 (e) のなかから語義としてふさわしいものをそれぞれ選びなさい。

1) ethanol   2) non-renewable   3) gasoline
4) bushel   5) automobile

(a) a form of petroleum

(b) a unit for measuring grains

(c) another word for a car

(d) a type of alcohol

(e) something that cannot be replaced once it is used

1st Listening ▶▶▶ まず VOA ニュースを聴きましょう。

SUMMARY CHECK

ニュースの概要として最もふさわしいものを下の 1) 〜 4) のなかから選びなさい。

1) There is growing concern in the U.S. about the dangers of ethanol.

2) Craig Turner's website has recently improved its analysis of ethanol and gasoline.

3) Farmers who sell their produce for ethanol production are concerned about a decrease in demand.

4) Although ethanol itself is a good product, the EPA is worried that some farmers are becoming too dependent on it.

2nd Listening

▶▶▶ もう一回 VOA ニュースを聴き、(　　　) を埋めましょう。

From VOA Learning English, this is the Agriculture Report.

Farmers in the United States are concerned about a (1.　　　) decrease in the use of ethanol. Ethanol is a (2.　　　) fuel made from plants, such as corn.

Last November, the Environmental Protection Agency proposed lowering the (3.　　　) amount of ethanol in the nation's gasoline (4.　　　). The requirement began in 2007 as part of a law meant to make the United States energy (5.　　　). The law required fuel manufactures to mix ethanol into their gasoline to reduce the use of non-renewable fuels. The amount of ethanol in the fuel (6.　　　) was to increase over time.

That was good news for corn (7.　　　) like Brian Duncan of Polo, Illinois. He thinks the proposed changes in ethanol requirements will (8.　　　) corn sales. Farmers enjoyed some of their best corn (9.　　　) in 2013. But the price of corn (10.　　　) from a high of more than seven dollars a bushel. Corn prices (11.　　　) in 2012. That year, a (12.　　　) of rain reduced the corn crop. Yet the (13.　　　) for corn in ethanol production (14.　　　).

Craig Turner works for a website called GrainAnalyst.com. He says the United States is using about nine percent (15.　　　) gasoline than it (16.　　　) in 2008. Mr. Turner says the reduced use of gasoline (17.　　　) the market does not need any more ethanol. He says less ethanol is needed as more energy-saving automobiles are being manufactured and (18.　　　). These vehicles, such as (19.　　　) or electric cars, use less fuel.

But farmers like Brian Duncan (20.　　　) on selling their corn to ethanol producers. He says farmers had been planning on the EPA continuing to require an increase in the use of "green" fuel.

For VOA Learning English, I'm Alex Villarreal.

Notes

☐ Environmental Protection Agency(= EPA)（米国）環境保護庁

TRUE OR FALSE?

1)〜5)のなかからニュースの内容として正しいものにはT、間違っているものにはFを選びなさい。

1) Ethanol cannot be made from corn.

2) A 2007 law required fuel manufacturers to stop mixing ethanol into gasoline.

3) The United States is using more gasoline now than it did in 2008.

4) Energy-saving automobiles are reducing the demand for gasoline.

5) Some farmers are disappointed that the Environmental Protection Agency may lower the required amount of ethanol in gasoline.

VOCABULARY BUILDING

下の語群の語を本文中で探して下線を引きなさい。そして、下の1)〜8)の英文の意味が通るように品詞・形などを変えたものを入れなさい。

1) Soy sauce is _____ from fermented soy beans.

2) Environmentalists are looking for ways to _____ atmospheric carbon dioxide levels.

3) One _____ of this job is that you can speak English and Chinese.

4) Going to a university far away from your home can help you to become more _____.

5) The _____ of caffeine in a typical cup of coffee is about 150 mg.

6) One feature of education in the 21st century is the increasing _____ of computers.

7) Smoking in public places is now against the _____ in several countries.

8) Some popular grain crops are wheat, _____, and barley.

| amount | corn | independent | law |
| lower | made | requirement | use |

USEFUL EXPRESSIONS

日本語に合うように（　　　）を埋めなさい。

1) 環境保護主義者たちは北極圏の氷の溶解について心配している。

   Environmentalists are (　　　) about the melting of ice in the Arctic.

2) 加工食品の異性化糖の使用を減らすことを栄養士は要求している。

   Nutritionists are calling for a (　　　) in the use of high-fructose corn syrup in processed foods.

3) 私たちのジャムには人工甘味料はまったく含まれず、すべて摘みたての果物で作られている。

   Our jams contain no artificial sweeteners and are all made (　　　) freshly-picked fruit.

4) アメリカ政府から提案された食品ラベルの変更は栄養成分が消費者により分かりやすくなるよう意図されている。

   The U.S. government's proposed changes to food labels are (　　　) to make nutritional information clearer to consumers.

TRANSLATIONS

日本語に合うように（　　　）の語句を並び替えて、一文を完成させなさい。

1) 1920年代の自動車と大量生産技術の発明がアメリカの生活様式に大きな変化をもたらした。

   The invention of the automobile and of mass production techniques in the 1920s (about / American / brought / changes / in / life / major / of / the / way).

   ....

2) 再生不能な燃料を自然エネルギーに替えることは長い年月を要する複雑なプロセスである。

   The replacement of (a / complex / energies / fuels / green / is / many / non-renewable / process / take / that / will / with / years).

   ....

15 | A New Way to Find Malaria Infections

新たなマラリア診断法

VOCABULARY

(a) 〜 (e) のなかから語義としてふさわしいものをそれぞれ選びなさい。

1) malaria   2) laser   3) costly

4) particle   5) parasite

(a) expensive

(b) a disease spread by mosquito bites

(c) light amplification by stimulated emission of radiation; a very narrow, powerful line of light

(d) an extremely small piece of something

(e) a plant or animal that lives on or in another living thing

1st Listening ▶▶▶ まず VOA ニュースを聴きましょう。

SUMMARY CHECK

ニュースの概要として最もふさわしいものを下の 1) 〜 4) のなかから選びなさい。

1) Rice University has set up a malaria testing center.

2) The *Proceedings of the National Academy of Sciences* has recently published many articles on malaria.

3) Laser technology will be key in advancing the diagnosis and treatment of malaria.

4) A new medical device uses a laser to test for malaria infection cheaply.

2nd Listening

▶▶▶ もう一回 VOA ニュースを聴き、(　　　) を埋めましょう。

From VOA Learning English, this is the Health Report.

Researchers have (1.　　　) a medical device which they say can recognize malaria infections in the human body. The laser (2.　　　) scanner is said to be the first device to (3.　　　) the disease without a blood test. The test is (4.　　　), does not require blood from the sick person, and appears to be (5.　　　) every time.

At present, doctors use costly (6.　　　) to test for malaria. The new test only needs a person to place a (7.　　　) on the laser device.

Dr. Dmitri Lopotko is (8.　　　) Rice University in Houston, Texas. He says the scanner works by (9.　　　) a very short pulse of light through the skin. The light comes from a low-powered laser. It shines on a very small particle called the hemozoin. The malaria parasite produces hemozoin when it (10.　　　) red blood cells. Hemozoin crystals are not found in blood cells that are (11.　　　) of the disease. As the laser (12.　　　) the crystals, they create small (13.　　　) inside infected cells. Dr. Lopotko says the bubbles (14.　　　), making a sound that scientists can hear and (15.　　　).

He says that in tests, the laser scanner was never (16.　　　). It also identified the malaria infection early, when treatment is important.

The device is easy to carry, and (17.　　　) on battery power. It costs about $10,000 to $20,000 to make. Dr. Lopotko (18.　　　) that each laser beam scanner could test more than 200,000 people a year. He says that means the cost of testing would be less than 50 (19.　　　) for each patient.

An (20.　　　) describing the malaria testing device was published in the journal *Proceedings of the National Academy of Sciences.*

For VOA Learning English, I'm Carolyn Presutti.

Notes
☐ Rice University ライス大学　　☐ hemozoin ヘモゾイン　　☐ crystal 結晶

TRUE OR FALSE?

1) ～ 5) のなかからニュースの内容として正しいものにはT、間違っているものにはFを選びなさい。

1) A new scanning device uses a laser beam to detect malaria infections in the human body.
2) The new device is accurate but a little painful.
3) Hemozoin is a particle that is present only in people infected with malaria.
4) The new device is very big and heavy.
5) The new device costs only about 50 cents.

VOCABULARY BUILDING

下の語群の語を本文中で探して下線を引きなさい。そして、下の1) ～ 8) の英文の意味が通るように品詞・形などを変えたものを入れなさい。

1) A GPS receiver is a _____ that gives you location and time information.
2) You've changed your hairstyle. I didn't _____ you at first!
3) To make a successful business, it is important to _____ your customers' needs.
4) We will give you an anesthetic, so the operation will be completely _____.
5) Mistakes made while operating machinery can be _____.
6) Providing adequate _____ care to an aging population is very difficult.
7) What you wrote was grammatically _____ but it wasn't very natural.
8) My doctor checked my blood pressure and _____.

| correct | costly | device | identify |
| medical | painless | pulse | recognize |

USEFUL EXPRESSIONS

日本語に合うように（　　　）を埋めなさい。

1) 日本では最近、かつては珍しかったたくさんの飲食物が比較的大きな町や都市で手に入れやすい。

   These days in Japan, a lot of formerly rare imported foods and drinks are (　　　) to obtain in larger towns and cities.

2) まもなく多くのエレベーターが太陽光発電で動くことになると期待されている。

   It is expected that soon many elevators will operate (　　　) solar power.

3) アメリカの地方の幹線道路は建設するのに1マイル1レーン当たり約1,000万ドルかかる。

   A highway in a U.S. rural area costs about 10 million dollars per lane per mile (　　　) construct.

4) 深刻な感染症であれば、感染が完全になくなるまで患者は隔離されなければならない。

   With some serious infectious diseases, patients have to be isolated until they are completely free (　　　) infection.

TRANSLATIONS

日本語に合うように（　　　）の語句を並び替えて、一文を完成させなさい。

1) レーザーの技術は手術や印刷のような多くの分野で使われている。

   Laser (and / as / fields / in / is / many / printing / such / surgery / technology / used).

2) マラリヤは貧困の原因であり経済発展の障害であると示唆する研究もある。

   Some research (a block / a cause / and / development / economic / is / malaria / of / poverty / suggests / that / to).

JPCA 本書は日本出版著作権協会（JPCA）が委託管理する著作物です。
複写（コピー）・複製、その他著作物の利用については、事前にJPCA（電
話 03-3812-9424、e-mail:info@e-jpca.com）の許諾を得て下さい。なお、
日本出版著作権協会 無断でコピー・スキャン・デジタル化等の複製をすることは著作権法上
http://www.e-jpca.com/ の例外を除き、著作権法違反となります。

All the Scripts © Voice of America

For a Better Future
Health & Environment Topics from VOA
未来のための健康と環境——〈カフェインと記憶力増進の関係性〉から〈太陽エネルギーの有効利用〉まで

2015 年 4 月 10 日　初版第 1 刷発行
2015 年 10 月 1 日　初版第 2 刷発行

編著者　　安浪誠祐／Richard S. Lavin

発行者　　森　信久
発行所　　株式会社　松 柏 社
　　　　　〒 102-0072　東京都千代田区飯田橋 1-6-1
　　　　　TEL 03 (3230) 4813（代表）
　　　　　FAX 03 (3230) 4857
　　　　　http://www.shohakusha.com
　　　　　e-mail: info@shohakusha.com

装　　幀　　小島トシノブ（NONdesign）
本文レイアウト　廣田清子＋ Office SunRa
組版・印刷・製本　シナノ書籍印刷株式会社

略号 = 703
ISBN978-4-88198-703-2
Copyright © 2015 by Seisuke Yasunami & Richard S. Lavin

本書を無断で複写・複製することを禁じます。
落丁・乱丁は送料小社負担にてお取り替え致します。